Sex, Dating, And

INTIMACY
IN & OUT

Master The Art Of Being A Confident Woman

Tabitha Ferguson

Table of Contents

Chapter 1:

7 Signs You're More Attractive Than You Think.

We feel conscious about ourselves every now and then. We are our own biggest critics. Finding flaws in ourselves sometimes leads to constructive criticism, which in turn leads to self-development. But sometimes, the constructive criticism might lead to a self-destructive reproach that will disturb the healthy and happy life you're living. It's normal to have self-doubts, wondering how people see us or what they think about us.

We live in a society where there is constant pressure to look your best self. People might point out our flaws and weaknesses, but what matters is how we emerge from it all. A study by Feynman in 2007 revealed that the way people see us determines how they will treat us. So, it's best if we remain confident and comfortable in our skin. Our appearances can either make or break the first impression of how people will perceive us. Research in 2016 by Lammers, Davis, Davidson, and Hogue revealed that first impressions could have a lasting effect on our relationship with the other person.

Many of us are used to being hard on ourselves. So it practically seems like a joke that anyone would find us attractive. Here are 7 signs that will confirm that you're more attractive than you think!

1. You rarely get compliments:

I know many of you wouldn't believe this but just hear me out first. Have you ever put on your most fabulous outfit, put on that sexy cologne, and dressed up all stunning from head to toe? You were confident enough that all eyes would be on you, and you will receive tons of compliments. But by the end of it all, you have hardly received any! Naturally, this would lead to you having some severe self-doubts about yourself. But you needn't worry. Psychology says that whenever we see a gorgeous person, we assume that he/she might have very high self-esteem. As a result, people rarely compliment those people. People also think that you already know how stunning you look, and you might be getting a lot of attention already. So, they avoid complimenting you too much. Instead of treating the scarcity of compliments as a bad thing, just maybe you are already the subject of many secret admirers.

2. The Compliments you get feel insincere:

Finally, you're receiving those compliments that you have been waiting for, for so long. But to your surprise, they sound apathetic and emotionless. You're confirmed now that you don't come off quite as attractive to other people. But we have a theory on this too. Suppose there is a gorgeous friend of yours. Do you constantly flatter them and gush about their appearance? You don't. You only compliment them if they're wearing a new outfit or changed their looks. The same happens to you. People think you already know how beautiful you are, so they don't pay much attention to the compliments they give you. The sole reason why the compliments sound so mundane and trivial. So, if you have been experiencing this, then you're more attractive than you think.

3. People get nervous around you:

Whenever you enter a room, you notice people suddenly being all nervous around you. This may happen because they're caught off guard by how gorgeous you look. They may feel pressured to make an excellent first impression since you've already made a perfect one on them. As a result, they try to hide their flaws in In front of you. They might become either too confident or underconfident. People tend to become awkward and nervous when they see other people as too attractive or too perfect.

4. You find yourself locking eyes with a lot of people:

We, humans, tend to stare at the desirable things we want. Research by the University of Oslo in 2015 found that your brain gives you a dopamine shot when you look at something pleasurable. While it may not always be the case that people staring at you might find you attractive. Sometimes it can just be a mistake, or maybe you have worn your shirt wrong, or there's something stuck on your teeth, but a lot of times, we stare and lock eyes with the people we find good-looking. So, if a person keeps staring at you even if you have caught them and passes a smile, it definitely means he likes what he's staring at.

5. People are surprised by your insecurities:

People might become shocked when you tell them about your complexes and insecurities. They think that since you're so gorgeous, you have nothing to worry about. But we all have our bad days where we go through self-doubts and low self-esteem. People wouldn't see this as such a problem because they would love to look like you and don't even notice the flaws you point out about yourself. Instead, they might become irritated when you complain about your issues because you look so self-confident and self-sufficient to them.

6. **People are often too polite or too unfriendly to you:**

You find people being either too optimistic or too pessimistic around you. They either might be too warm and friendly or too harsh and rude when you first meet them. The truth is, people, tend to react strongly to the people they find attractive. Some people might find excuses to spend time with you and praise you, while others may sound too petty around you. This might also be because of the jealousy they may feel towards you. A positive person will always see you as an equal and will always treat you with a polite and friendly attitude.

7. **People are interested in you:**

You might feel people asking a lot of questions about you and getting to know you better. They carry the conversation and like talking to you from time to time. Even though your communication skills are pretty average, they would still speak to you with the same interest. This is because they might think that you would have a great personality. After all, you have a pretty face. They would become compromising and would jump at the first opportunity to help you. We tend to be friendlier and more generous to the people subconsciously we find attractive. By helping you, they want to look good in your eyes too.

Conclusion:

You need to look past your insecurities, embrace your flaws, and accept the characteristics that people value in you. Don't forget that in the end, a good heart always wins over good looks. Don't become a victim of societal pressure and mould yourself into a perfect and flawless human being. There is nothing more attractive than appreciating yourself with all the good and the bad and knowing your worth. Find happiness in being vulnerable and weak, through the tough and challenging times. Life is a roller coaster ride, so you shouldn't have a need to feel perfect all the time!

Chapter 2:

6 Behaviours That Keep You Single

Dating may not be as easy as it is shown in all those romantic Hollywood movies. There is so much more than appearance and stability in dating someone. And when you are old enough to be involved with someone, you sometimes find yourself uninterested. You think about how everyone your age has already started dating while you are back there eating junk and watching Netflix. It might appear to you that being in a relationship is tiresome, and you stop trying for it. Everyone has a different preference when it comes to finding someone for themselves. You tend to look for someone that matches your knight in the shining armor, which makes it hard for you to find someone you need.

Be true to you yourself while finding someone to date. Looking for someone with the expectation that you are rich and handsome would be foolish. It would be best if you worked on yourself more than that. Make yourself ease around with people but no so much that they start to get annoyed. Don't get in your way.

1. **Trust Is Essential**

Trusting each other is an important factor for dating someone. If you don't trust your partner even in the slightest, then nothing will matter. You will constantly doubt each other. Both of you will eventually fall apart if there is no trust. And if you have trust issues, it will be difficult for you to find someone worthy. But, if you trust too quickly, then it's only natural that you will break your bubble of expectations. Be friendly. Try to get to know them properly before making any assumptions about them. You don't want to go around hesitating about everything. Find yourself a reliable partner that trusts you too.

2. Too Many Expectations

Expecting too much from your partner will lead to only one thing. It leads towards Disappointment. It would help if you let them be. Don't expect things to go your way always. Your knight in the shining armor may be a bookworm because people find love in the most unexpected places. It doesn't always mean to keep no expectations at all. To keep the expectations low. You will get surprised constantly when you don't know what's coming your way. Don't let people cloud your judgment, and keep high standards about a relationship. Everyone has their share of ups and downs. Comparison with others will not be suitable for your relationship.

3. Have Self-Confidence

One has to respect itself before anything else can. You have to have self-esteem in you for people to take you seriously. It is true "you can't love someone unless you learn to love yourself first." You tend to feel insecure about yourself. Everything around you seems too perfect for you. And you constantly think that your partner will stop loving you one day. That fear of yours will get you nowhere. Try to give yourself as much care you can. It doesn't hurt to be loved.

4. Don't Overthink

You found a guy, and He seems to be excellent. But you start to overthink it. Eventually, you let go. That is what you shouldn't have done. Just try to go with the flow sometimes. Don't try too hard for it. Go for it the easy way. Overthinking will lead you to make up scenarios that never happened. Just let it be and see where it goes. Be easy so people can approach you. Think, don't overthink.

5. Involving Too Many People

When you initially start dating, you get nervous. People get help from their friends sometimes. But it is not necessary to get every move through them. Involving them in everything will only get your partner get uncomfortable and get you frustrated. People tend to give a lot of opinions of their own. You will get confused. So, it is good to keep these things to yourself. Be mindful in giving them a brief report from time to time. However, keep them at a reasonable distance.

6. Giving Up Too Quickly

If it doesn't work initially, it does not mean that it will never work. Patience is an essential element when it comes to dating anyone. Don't give up too quickly. Try to make it work until it's clear that it won't. Give it your all. Compromise on things you can. Because if both of you are not willing to compromise, it will not work between you both. It will work out in the end if it's meant to be. Don't push it if it's not working too.

Conclusion

It is hard; it keeps going at a pace. But all you must need is that spark that keeps it alive. Make it work until it doesn't. Go for it all. Make commitments only when you are sure about your choice. And be true to your words. Who wants to be single forever?

Chapter 3:

8 Signs A Boy Wants To Kiss You

You like him, and you're hoping he has the same feelings for you, too. Hanging out with him is such a pleasure, and you always have a great time together. It's easy to tell that he enjoys your company, but how do you know if he only likes you as a friend?

Not knowing whether or not someone you like has feelings for you can be agonizing. One way to know if he likes you as more than just a friend is if he shows some signs he wants to kiss you. You won't need to find the courage to ask him outright. If he wants to kiss you, it will be clear how he feels about you.

Here are 8 ways to tell if a guy wants to kiss you.

1. He's acting flirty

If he usually behaves one way and then all of a sudden seems to act differently (in a smiley, giggly kind of way), then he's flirting with you! His attention is undividedly on you. His eyes are filled with the look of happy mischief because he has kissed you on his mind.

2. He stares at your lips

As you speak to him, he stares at your mouth or keeps glancing down at your lips. He might be doing it deliberately, hoping that you'll get the hint that he wants to plant one on you. Or, he might not even know that he's doing it. But because he's thinking about kissing you, his focus will keep going to your lips.

3. He makes a comment about your lips or mouth

He might also comment on your lips, such as, "you've got the cutest lips" or "what's the color of this lipstick you're wearing?" this is one of the sure signs a guy wants to kiss you. He definitely likes you and is going to make his move soon.

4. Lingering eye contact

He doesn't just look at you, but he gazes into your eyes. If the guy you like starts looking at you the same way you look at a chocolate-covered donut (if you're into that sort of thing), then you can be positive that he likes you as more than just a friend.

5. He makes physical contact

If he's planning on kissing you, he might break the ice by touching you a little in subtle ways. A stroke of your arm, a hand on the cheek, and even a one-armed side hug are all ways he will get you used to make contact with him before he gets even closer.

6. He seems a little nervous

He might normally be confident around you, but if he starts acting nervous, clumsy, or distracted, it may be one of the signs he wants to kiss you. He might have a feeling that you like him, but his not knowing for sure might make him afraid of your reaction when he does try to kiss you. So don't be surprised if he seems to have lost his confidence all of a sudden.

7. He falls silent suddenly

Falling silent is a similar sign of nervousness before an impending kiss. He's probably busy thinking about how, where, or when he's going to make his move. He might be thinking, "is this the perfect moment for our first kiss?"

Building up the courage to finally show a girl how you feel can be scary. It's no wonder he's lost in his thoughts.

8. His voice softens

Psychologists say that when a guy starts using a softer tone of voice, it is one sign that he wants to kiss you. For some reason, whispered voices go along with passion and proximity. I mean, speaking loudly or abruptly isn't sexy, is it? So it makes sense.

If his tone of voice changes, know that he's attracted to you and wants to kiss you.

Knowing if a guy has feelings for you might not always be easy. But if he does want to change the status of your friendship, one of the ways you'll know for sure is if he shows signs he wants to kiss you. So, if you notice any of the signs described above, all you have to do is be prepared for your first kiss and your new romance.

Chapter 4:
9 Ways to Achieve Harmony In Your Professional Relationships

Offices are a microcosm of humanity. They are a mix of all types of people, with all types of personalities, quirks, goals, and challenges, so for everyone to get along beautifully, it takes effort.

You probably remember a time in your career when a "clash of personalities" corrupted a productive working environment. You can prevent this from happening and create harmony in your office with these nine simple practices.

1. Say Thank You

These two little words may be the most powerful when it comes to creating happiness and harmony. People work hard and take pride in their accomplishments but can feel overlooked. Taking time to acknowledge even the smallest achievement can make a person feel valued. Say thank you not only for the big job they've completed, say thank you when they open the door, offer to get you coffee or invite you to lunch. Offer a genuine thank you every day.

2. Notice The Little Things

If a co-worker or employee is happy at their job, they will go out of their way to add a little extra to their commitment. They might take on an extra assignment or stay late to help out with an uncompleted project. Or they may do subtle things like clean up the kitchen area or edit a company document on which they noticed errors. The more you notice and offer thanks for these little "extras," the more you will build happiness and harmony in the office, and the more motivated your co-workers will become to continue looking for ways to improve the business.

3. Avoid Idle Gossip

Gossip can tarnish office harmony. It might seem entertaining at the moment, but underneath, it builds distrust. Resentments build, people begin to wonder if they are the ones being gossiped about, and chasms open. Establish a "no-gossip policy" and enforce it. Extend your no-gossip policy for events outside the office as well, such as happy hours, company outings, or holiday parties, where relaxed environments and alcohol can loosen inhibitions.

4. Maintain An Open-Door Policy

Establish an open environment for discussion by creating a "come to me anytime" system. Be open to suggestions, complaints, or discussions without judgment. Because people come from different backgrounds and experiences, everyone has their way of looking at things. By listening, you can understand what others see from their point of view instead of your own. When people feel open to talk, you can nip problems in the bud before they escalate into real obstacles or unearth substantial opportunities you may not have noticed before.

5. Create A Team Environment

Hold regular meetings with the entire office and empower co-workers to take "ownership" of the business. If they feel their opinions and insights hold value, they will be more likely to use their talents and creativity to help build the business as a whole. Instead of taking orders, they will work together to look for ways to improve.

6. Offer To Help

Jump in and be hands-on yourself. Whenever you are stuck, overworked, or faced with a major deadline, you know how you appreciate a helping hand. It may take a little extra effort, but pitch in to help your co-workers over a hump.

7. Socialize Outside Of Work

Build friendships and harmonies outside of work with casual outings. Plan a monthly happy hour, establish a yearly barbeque picnic or kick up a friendly competition with a bowling or softball tournament. The relaxed environment will create bonds that go deeper than the company's latest accounting policies.

8. Get Everyone Involved

Every employee likes to be informed and in the loop, even if the news has nothing to do with them. Keeping an employee informed is an effortless way to make them feel appreciated and valuable in your business. Beyond this, you should always trust your team and be confident in delegating work to them – nobody likes working under a boss who micromanages everything they do and gives them no individuality in their work. Getting everyone involved is an easy way to please even the lowest-level employees and ensure that your office has harmony.

9. Communicate

Communication is crucial for any work environment. Every boss needs to have an open-door policy and be willing to talk to an employee at any time; on the other hand, every employee needs to be sure that they reach out and talk to higher-level employees. Learning is crucial in any office, and the central way for workers to learn is through communication. Beyond communication about work, occasional non-work-related talk is also important – it's a bad sign if you don't know anything about your fellow worker outside of work. Ask someone about their family or hobbies or whatever it may be; these small talk conversations may seem meaningless but are important for building harmony in the workplace.

Chapter 5:

How Will You Choose To Live Your Life?

How will you choose to live your life? This is something that only you have the power to decide.

We all want different things. As individuals, we are all unique and we have our own ideas about what it means to live a meaningful life. Some treasure family, friends, and relationships above all else, while others prioritise money, material things, careers, and productivity. There is no right or wrong to pursue or place any of these things on a pedestal. If your dream is to build a multi-billion dollar company, then go ahead and chase that dream. If you prioritise just being as stress-free as possible, to do as little work as you can, well you can choose to structure your life in such a way as well. As long as it works for you and that you are happy doing so, I would say go for it.

Sure, your priorities might change as you get older and wiser. Embrace that change. We are not always met to move in a linear fashion in life. We should learn to live like water, being fluid, ever-changing, ever-growing, ever-evolving. Our interests, priorities, passions, all change as we move from one stage of life to the next.

Some only realise that they might want to focus on relationships at a certain point in their lives, some might only want to start a family when they reach a certain age. The point is that we never truly know when is the time when we might feel ready to do something, as much as well tell ourselves that we will know.

The best thing we can do for ourselves right now, in this very moment, is to do what we think is best for us right now, and then to make tweaks and adjustments along the way as we travel down that road faithfully.

Trying to plan and control every aspects of our lives rarely ever works out how we imagined it. You see, life will give us lemons, but it can also give us durians. We might get thrown off the road through unexpected changes. Things that challenge our beliefs and our priorities. Health issues, family tragedies, financial meltdowns, natural disasters, these are things that we can never plan for. We may either choose to come out of these things with a clearer plan for our next phase of life, or we may choose to give up and not try anymore.

All of us have the power to choose how we want to live our lives in this very moment. The worst thing you can do right now is not know what your priorities are and to just cruise through life without having at least a short-term vision on what you want to get out of it.

Take the time to reflect every single day to work on that goal, however scary or simple it may be. Never take your eye off the post and just keep traveling down that path until you reach a fork in the road.

Chapter 6:

8 Ways To Make The Sex Good

Has your sex life gone stale? Between kids, work, financial pressures, and all the other stressful things, steamy sex may seem like nothing but a fantasy.

Sex isn't just fun, but it's healthy for you too. Every orgasm releases a burst of oxytocin, which instantly improves your mood. Regular rolls in the hay could also improve your heart health, improve your self-esteem, reduce stress and depression, and help you sleep better. As little as only snuggling together underneath the sheets also make you feel closer to your partner and can enhance your sense of intimacy.

If you're stuck in a sexual rut, trust me, you're not alone. While dry spells are expected in any relationship, it's still no consolation for couples experiencing one. The more we get used to someone, the less exciting sex becomes, as familiarity is the death of sex drive. Treating sexual problems is easier now than ever before.

Here are some quick tips to help you reignite the passion your sex life is lacking.

1. **Stop Feeling Insecure About Your Body**

It really doesn't matter if you haven't lost the baby weight, your specific body parts aren't as high as they used to be, or you have a pimple the size of an egg; it doesn't matter at all. When you're in bed and making love, your partners are not worried about any of your imperfections. To him, you're still the sexiest lady he fell in love with. Besides, it would be best if you understood that his body isn't perfect either. He might have a large belly or a body full of hair. But he doesn't let it get in the way of a good time, and you shouldn't either.

2. Mark A Date

Scheduling sex might sound controlling and not at all fun, but sometimes planning is in order. You book time in your calendar for many things, so why not do the same to prioritize sex? You have to make some room for it and push it forward. Reconnecting with your partner will remind you why you got attracted to him in the first place. Once you have made that sex appointment, the anticipation can be almost as titillating as the event. So, trade some racy texts or leave a sultry voicemail on his cell.

3. Use Lubrication

Often, the vaginal dryness can lead to painful sex, which can, in turn, lead to flagging libido and growing relationship tensions. To avoid any pain during sex or hurting yourself resulting from it, use lubricating liquids and gels. This will make the sex painless and turn on both of you more and more.

4. Practice Touching

Sex therapists use sensate focus techniques that can help you re-establish physical intimacy without feeling pressured. Many of the self-help books and educational videos offer many variations on such exercises. You can also ask your partner to touch you in a manner that you would like to be touched by them, or ask them how they want to be touched. This will give you an idea of the range of pressure from gentle to firm that you should use.

5. Try Different Positions

Sometimes, couples get bored by trying the same 2-3 positions over and over again. Searching and trying new positions will definitely spice up your love life. Developing a repertoire of different sexual positions can enhance your experience of lovemaking and add interest and help you overcome problems. For example, when a man enters his partner from behind, the increased stimulation to the G-spot can help a woman reach orgasm faster.

6. Write Down Your Fantasies

This exercise can help you explore endless possibilities that you think might turn on you and your partner. It could be anything, from reading an erotic book to watching an aroused scene from a movie or TV show that turned you on, you could re-enact them with your partner. Similarly, you could ask your partner about their fantasies and help them fulfill them. This activity is also helpful for people with low desires.

7. Do Kegel Exercises

Both men and women should improve their sexual fitness by exercising their pelvic floor muscles. To do these exercises, tighten the muscle you would use while trying to stop urine in midstream. Hold the contraction for two or three seconds, then release. Repeat 10 times of five sets a day. These exercises can be done anywhere while driving, sitting at your desk, or standing in a check-out line. At home, women may use vaginal weights to add muscle resistance.

8. Try To Relax

Do something soothing and relaxing together before having sex instead of jumping right into it (not that you can't do that), such as playing a game, watching a movie, or having a nice candlelight dinner.

Conclusion

Lack of communication is often what leads to sex droughts in a relationship. Even if you are sexually mismatched, you can get creative and fix those inequities. Stress and busyness of life, among other factors, can also affect sexual intimacy, but there are fruitful ways to overcome setbacks. Don't let fear or embarrassment stop you from trying new stuff. Tap into something simple to get back on track.

Chapter 7:
Setting Too High Expectations

Today we're going to talk about the topic of setting too high expectations. Expectations about everything from work, to income, to colleagues, friends, partners, children, family. Hopefully by the end of this video I will be able to help you take things down a notch in some areas so that you don't always get disappointed when things don't turn out the way you expect it to.

Let's go one by one in each of these areas and hopefully we can address the points that you are actively engaged in at the moment.

Let's begin with work and career. Many of us have high expectations for how we want our work life to be. How we expect our companies and colleagues to behave and the culture that we are subjected to everyday. More often that not though, companies are in the business of profit-making and cutting costs. And our high expectations may not meet reality and we might end up getting let down. What I would recommend here is that we not set these expectations of our colleagues and bosses, but rather we should focus on how we can best navigate through this obstacle course that is put in front of us. We may want to focus instead on how we can handle ourselves and our workload. If however we find that we just can't shake off this expectations that we want from working in a company, maybe we want to look elsewhere to companies that have a work culture that suits our personality. Maybe one that is more vibrant and encourages freedom of expression.

Another area that we should address is setting high expectations of our partners and children. Remember that we are all human, and that every person is their own person. Your expectations of them may not be their expectations of themselves. When you impose such an ideal on them, it may be hard for them to live up to. Sure you should expect your partner to be there for you and for your children to behave a certain way.

But beyond that everyone has their own personalities and their own thoughts and ideas. And what they want may not be in line with what we want for them. Many a times for Asian parents, we expect our kids to get good grades, get into good colleges, and maybe becoming a doctor or lawyer one day. But how many of us actually understand what our kids really want? How many of us actually listen to what our kids expect of themselves? Maybe they really want to be great at music, or a sport, or even finance. Who's to say what's actually right? We should learn to trust others and let go of some of our own expectations of them and let them become whoever they want to be.

The next area I want to talk about is simply setting too high expectations of yourself. Many times we have an ideal of who we want to be - how we want to look, how we want our bodies to look, and how we want our bank statement to look, amongst many others. The danger here is when we set unrealistic expectations as to when we expect these things to happen. Remember most things in life takes time to happen. The sooner you realise that you need more time to get there, the easier it will be on yourself. When we set unrealistic timelines, while it may seem ideal to rush through the process to get results fast, more often than not we are left disappointed when we don't hit them. We then get discouraged and may even feel like a failure or give up the whole process entirely. Wouldn't it be better if we could give ourselves more time for nature to work its magic? Assuming you follow the steps that you have laid out and the action plans you need to take, just stretch this timeline out a little farther to give yourself more breathing room. If you feel you are not progressing as fast as you had hoped, it is okay to seek help and to tweak your plans as they go along. Don't ever let your high expectations discourage you and always have faith and trust in the process even when it seems hard.

One final thing I want to talk about is how we can shift from setting too high expectations to one of setting far-out goals instead. There is a difference. Set goals that serve to motivate you and inspire you to do things rather than ones that are out of fear. When we say we expect something, we immediately set ourselves up for disappoint. However if we tell ourselves that we really want something, or that we want to achieve something that is of great importance to us, we shift to a goal-oriented mindset. One that is a lot healthier. We no longer fear the deadline creeping up on us. We instead continually work on getting there no matter how long it takes. That we tell ourselves we will get there no matter what, no matter how long. The key is to keep at it consistently and never give up.

Having the desire to work at an Apple store as a retail specialist, I never let myself say that I expect apple to hire me by a certain time otherwise I am never pursuing the job ever again. Rather I tell myself that being an Apple specialist is my dream job and that I will keep applying and trying and constantly trying to improve myself until Apple has no choice but to hire me one day. A deadline no longer bothers me anymore. While I wait for them to take me in, I will continue to pursue other areas of interest that will also move my life forward rather than letting circumstances dictate my actions. I know that I am always in control of my own ship and that I will get whatever I put my mind to eventually if I try hard enough.

So with that I challenge each and every one of you to be nicer to yourselves. Lower your lofty expectations and focus on the journey instead of the deadline. Learn to appreciate the little things around you and not let your ego get in the way.

I hope you learned something today, take care and I'll see you in the next one.

Chapter 8:

9 Signs an Introvert Likes You

A lot of people out there are conscious to know about the tell-tale signs that reveal if an Introvert Likes You or not. You are probably unsure if someone you know has a secret crush on you and you are eager to find out so that you can reciprocate those feelings, or maybe you want to be find out - out of mere curiosity.

Well, I want to first say that because there are many different kinds of introverts, we may not be able to cover all aspects of it. Some introverts like to be alone in their own comfort zones while others like to hang out with their inner circle of close friends and relatives. But basically an introvert is generally shy and more reserved by nature. They are usually more quiet and may seem like they have built up a little wall around them in the initial meetings you have with them.

In today's video, we are going into 9 specific signs than an Introvert Likes You. Hopefully this will shed a brighter light on this topic and bring you some lightbulb moments. So without any further delay, let's get right into it.

Number one
They will Try to Open up

Introverts are shy creatures that look for soul connection like a meeting of minds. So when an introvert likes you, they will try to open up, they will try to share their thoughts and feelings with you. They will tell you about that one best day of their life and they will tell you how they feel about themselves asking you, do you feel the same way?

So if an introvert overshares with you then you can take it as a plus point as they don't tell these things just to anyone. They tell you these things because you are special to them and they want you to share your world of thoughts too.

Number two
They Know A Lot About You

You might be amazed at this one and might be thinking, how can an introvert know that much about me so quickly? Ahmm, never underestimate their researching skills, just saying. If an introvert likes you then they could potentially look you up on social media, they might check out your posts to get to know who you are as a person a little more. They do their own behind-the-scenes search because they may be too shy to ask you in person, or they might do so to feel that they feel like they may know more about you before committing to liking you. So if they know these little details about you then there is a high chance that they do indeed like you.

Number three
They Will Be First To View Or Like Whatever You Post On Social Media

This one also comes under the previous point. If an introvert likes you, they might be the first to like your post on social media because they may be too shy to message you directly or tell you in person that they find you interesting. An introvert will leave breadcrumbs behind to show that they are interested in you. So yeah, you gotta check if they are doing it or not.

Number four
They Look At You More Than Usual People

If an introvert likes you then they will surely check you out. Whenever they come in front of you or if you are sitting in a group then that introvert will look at you like more than once, without making you feel uncomfortable. Yes! They have this talent. So if you catch them looking at you, then they are probably into you.

Number five
Laughing Nervously

If an Introvert likes you then they might shutter or blush in your presence as well as laugh nervously. They can also get tongue-tied while talking to you. Want to know the reason? Let me tell you. When an introvert talks to you, they are actually out of their comfort zone, so that's why they appear hyper-alert. They are putting themselves out there. Give them the space to be themselves if they appear to be acting this way.

Number six
Immediately Answer your Call Or They Call You

Introverts generally don't like taking calls. It would not be wrong to say that they let all calls go to the voicemail unless it's the call from their food delivery guy. So if an introvert picks up your calls or calls you to talk to you then they might be head over heels over you.

Number seven
Inviting You To Hangouts

Here, I would go back to the first point where I said, introverts don't share their private world with a normal person. Introverts don't go out much but still, they have some favorite places like a coffee shop, a park that makes them feel good, or a hiking trail. So if an introvert takes you to these kinds of places, it means they want to share some part of what makes them feel good.

Number eight
They Step Out Of Their Comfort Zone

This is the most that an introvert can do for you. Do you imagine how difficult it is to step out of your comfort zone? Not everyone can do it except for the person who likes you unconditionally. So if an Introvert likes you, they would love to go to parties, or in a music festival only if they know you would be there. They can stay up late at night just to talk to you and to spend some time with you.

Number nine
Writing "Love Messages"

Now, you might be thinking if a person writes us a love letter then it's an obvious thing that they like us, how is it a sign then? Let me tell you how. Actually, an introvert's love message is different from others.

They write things like, hey, how are you? How's your day going? Now, these things are common for an extrovert, they can ask these things to anyone but for an introvert, these messages are like love letters. As you know, introverts don't like talking much face to face so they explain their feelings by writing you a letter or sending you a text.

And writing is the apple pie of introverts. In writing, they can explain how they feel about you without being deficient of words but they will not do it. Introverts!! So if you are getting this kind of message or letters from an introvert, then it's an obvious thing that they like you.

So that's it, guys, we are done with our today's topic of nine Signs an Introvert Likes You. Now, it's time for you to share your thoughts. What do you think about these signs? Have you got your answer yet or not? And if you are an introvert then let us know if there are some additional things to help others. If you got value from this video then smash the like button and don't forget to subscribe to our channel as we will be talking about some amazing topics in the future. See you soon!

Chapter 9:

9 Signs of a Toxic Relationship

Before getting into the video, let's talk about what's a toxic relationship? Dr. Lillian Glass, a California-based psychology expert defines the toxic relationship as "any relationship [between two people who] don't support each other, where there's conflict and one seeks to undermine the other, where there's competition, where there's disrespect and a lack of cohesiveness."

Signs of toxic relationships are all around us. The question is how do we know if we have one? And what are the exact signs of such a relationship? In this video, I'm going to tell you 9 main signs of a toxic relationship. So let's get right into it.

Main

1. Unhealthy Communication Patterns

Passive aggressiveness, aggressive or bullying styles of conversations that your partner engages with you could be a clear sign that something isn't right between the two of you. The relationship can turn toxic very quickly when either partner feels guilted into responding in a submissive way to please the other. Furthermore bad communication can also lead to avoiding talking to your partner. Instead of treating you with love and compassion, if your partner has animosity, criticism, sarcasm, and egoism

37

in most of his conversations with you, then it can lead to hatred and thus poison the relationship. We all want a partner who can speak to us with kindness and understanding rather than someone who speaks to us in a threat-like manner.

2.   Habits or Cycles of Cheating and lying

If you feel that your partner is cheating on you or lying to you, it will damage your trust in your partner and may also harm the relationship. Once trust is lost, it is very difficult to get it back. You may start to trust your partner in days or months, but the possibility always seems fragile. Relationships with distrust can turn good partners into jealous or suspicious people. Sometimes even your partner's unforgettable compromises can't repair trust if it is badly broken. So, if for some reason you can't trust your partner then the relationship is definitely toxic.

3.   Your Loved Ones Strongly Disapproves of Your Partner

What people close to you think of your partner is one of the most important factors in determining whether the relationship is beneficial or one that could be toxic. So, make sure to pay close attention to what your friends, family, and loved ones are saying about your partner.

Your family and friends always want you to be safe and happy, so if they strongly dislike your partner then there must be a strong reason behind it. They may be able to see red flags in them that you might have otherwise overlooked that may point towards something toxic brewing.

That reason or some hateful reactions of your loved ones against your partner can indicate that the relationship is not good for you.

4. Over-Dependency On Your Partner

It has been noted by several personality experts that those who are the least self-sufficient (but also most self-critical) tend to be the most toxic partners. Sometimes this is a symptom of an underlying relationship problem. Sometimes it is not. But when a partner is absent-minded or disinterested in "self-care", that can be a red flag.

5. Constant Fears of Being Judged

Signs of toxic relationships can also include the feeling like you are constantly being judged. You may wonder why you always feel like you need to be on your best behavior. Or, you may think that you always get in trouble with your partner. Some partners can even pick fights as a way of getting back at their relationship - and then some feel like nothing's ever going right.

6. Feeling like you are being taken advantage of

One of the most important signs of toxic relationship behavior is feeling like you're being exploited. You may feel like you're not really treated with care or value. Perhaps you question whether or not you are important enough. You may worry that your partner sees you as someone they can take for granted.

In fact, one of the core dynamics of toxic relationships is that the less valuable you feel, the less valuable your partner will feel. When you have a deep, internal belief that you are not significant, it can lead to behaviors that are meant to hurt you.

7. You Are Always Defending Your Partner

One classic sign of toxic relationship behavior is when you find yourself defending your partner against charges of hurting you or you feel guilty and always come first to apologize to your partner but you are not sure why.

When the lines of communication between you and your partner start to break down, you may find yourself defending your partner instead of talking to solve problems. When you and your partner argue, you may also hear your partner say things like "you just need to learn to get along with people," "your problem is with you, not with me" or "you just want to ruin my life." Such behavior is enough to call the relationship toxic.

8. All the compromise comes from you

Nobody can manage a good relationship with a partner if they are the only one doing all compromise, work, and love.

A good relationship can only be built with the cooperation of both life partners. However, if you do everything while your partner does nothing and never gives the relationship a better chance to improve, then, of course, the relationship is toxic to you.

9. Your Partner Suffers From Addictions

The use of drugs, especially alcohol or (maybe) cigarettes, has a devastating effect on all relationships and is a major reason for leaving relationships. If your partner is addicted to drugs, and you think you can't solve the problem then make sure to provide him/her medical help. But if he/she is not ready at all to get rid of drugs and drinks too much alcohol regularly, you should consider the relationship toxic.

Closing

So that's it. We are done with our today's topic.

Remember that if you feel that you are in a toxic relationship, don't forget to seek help. Consult your friends and family, be open to their opinions and don't be afraid to end the relationship if it indeed turns out to be toxic. Remember that we only have one life to live and we deserve to be with a partner that can care and love us unconditionally in all the right ways.

Now it's your turn to share your thoughts. Do you know about any other signs of a toxic relationship? Let us know in the comments below. If you got value then hit the like and subscribe button.

Chapter 10:

What To Do When You Have Thoughts of Breaking Up

It's not always easy deciding if you should break up with your partner: You probably care about them and have many great memories together. But there could be real issues in the relationship that make you wonder if it's best to end things. Whatever outcome you settle on, however, it's a good idea to first ask yourself a few questions so you can be sure it's the right decision for you.

"Breaking up with your partner is the best thing to do if you feel like you're not happy anymore, and the relationship is just pulling you down instead of pushing you up.

Here are some things to think about before ending your relationship, according to experts.

1. Is There Anyone Influencing My Decision?

If you're seriously considering breaking up with your partner, it's wise to take a moment to think about what — or, more specifically, who — might be influencing you toward this decision. Is your mom insisting you'd be better off without them? Does your best friend swear that splitting up is your best option? Although people's opinions can be a good guiding force, at the end of the day, this is your choice, not theirs.

2. Do We Hold the Same Core Values?

When you and your partner first got together, you might have initially bonded because you have similar interests. But if you're now at a place where you're thinking of taking the next steps or breaking up, it's worth asking yourself if the two of you align on values, too. "Preferences in daily life will change, but core values will likely not change. "You could feel like it is time to break up with your partner because those [incompatible] core values are showing themselves."

3. Would I Want My Child to Be With Someone Like My Partner?

It may seem like a strange thing to consider if starting a family isn't on the horizon, but it can be an effective litmus test to picture how you'd feel if your child were with someone like your partner. "This will trigger a reality check — would you want your children to spend the rest of their lives with the same kind of person as your partner? "If your answer is no, then take it as a sign that you are heading in the right direction ending the relationship."

4. Is This A Pattern for Me?

Are you someone who starts thinking of breaking up with your partner a few months in each time you're in a relationship? Do you start losing interest at about the one-year mark? Ask yourself whether this is a genuine impulse or if it's just a pattern for you. "Is the reason I desire to break up with someone unique to this person, or would it apply to multiple people?" Clara Artschwager, "If it applies to more than one person, this is often indicative of a larger limiting pattern in relationships."

Are you scared of getting too close to someone? Are you afraid of commitment? Reflecting on these things can help with your decision.

Chapter 11:

6 Ways To Attract Anything You Want In Life

It is common human nature that one wants whatever one desires in life. People work their ways to get what they need or want. This manifestation of wanting to attract things is almost in every person around us. A human should be determined to work towards his goal or dreams through sheer hard work and will. You have to work towards it step by step because no matter what we try or do, we will always have to work for it in the end. So, it is imperative to work towards your goal and accept the fact that you can't achieve it without patience and dedication.

We have to start by improving ourselves day by day. A slight change a day can help us make a more considerable change for the future. We should feel the need to make ourselves better in every aspect. If we stay the way we are, tomorrow, we will be scared of even a minor change. We feel scared to let go of our comfort zone and laziness. That way, either we or our body can adapt to the changes that make you better, that makes you attract better.

1. **Start With Yourself First**

We all know that every person is responsible for his own life. That is why people try to make everything revolves around them. It's no secret that everyone wants to associate with successful, healthy, and charming people. But, what about ourselves? We should also work on ourselves to become the person others would admire. That is the type of person people love. He can also easily attract positive things to himself. It becomes easier to be content with your desires. We need to get ourselves together and let go of all the things we wouldn't like others doing.

2. Have A Clear Idea of Your Wants

Keeping in mind our goal is an easy way to attract it. Keep reminding yourself of all the pending achievements and all the dreams. It helps you work towards it, and it enables you to attract whatever you want. Make sure that you are aware of your intentions and make them count in your lives. You should always make sure to have a crystal-clear idea of your mindset, so you will automatically work towards it. It's the most basic principle to start attracting things to you.

3. Satisfaction With Your Achievements

It is hard to stop wanting what you once desired with your heart, but you should always be satisfied with anything you are getting. This way, when you attract more, you become happier. So, it is one of the steps to draw things, be thankful. Be thankful for what you are getting and what you haven't. Every action has a reason for itself. It doesn't mean just to let it be. Work for your goals but also acknowledge the ones already achieved by you in life. That way you will always be happy and satisfied.

4. Remove Limitations and Obstacles

We often limit ourselves during work. We have to know that there is no limit to working for what you want when it comes to working for what you want. You remove the obstacles that are climbing their way to your path. It doesn't mean to overdo yourselves, but only to check your capability. That is how much pressure you can handle and how far you can go in one go. If you put your boundaries overwork, you will always do the same amount, thus, never improving further. Push yourself a little more each time you work for the things you want in life.

5. Make Your Actions Count

We all know that visualizing whatever you want makes it easier to get. But we still cannot ignore the fact that it will not reach us unless we do some hard work and action. Our actions speak louder than words, and they speak louder than our thoughts. So, we have to make sure that our actions are built of our brain image. That is the way you could attract the things you want in life. Action is an essential rule for attracting anything you want in life.

6. Be Optimistic About Yourselves

Positivity is an essential factor when it comes to working towards your goals or dreams. When you learn to be optimistic about almost everything, you will notice that everything will make you satisfied. You will attract positive things and people. Negative vibes will leave you disappointed in yourself and everyone around you. So, you will have to practice positivity. It may not be easy at first while everyone around you is pushing you to negativity. That is where your test begins, and you have to prove yourself to them and yourself. And before you know it, you are attracting things you want.

Conclusion

Everyone around us wants to attract what they desire, but you have to start with yourself first. You only have to focus on yourself to achieve what you want. And attracting things will come naturally to you. Make sure you work for your dreams and goals with all your dedication and determination. With these few elements, you will be attracting anything you want.

Chapter 12:

Why You Should Practice Safe Sex During Dating and Relationships

Before you decide to have sex, or if you are already having sex, you need to know how to stay healthy. Even if you think you know everything you need to know about sex, take a few minutes and read on. Your doctor wants to make sure you know the facts.

Important Reminders:

- No one should ever be forced to have sex! If you are ever forced to have sex, it's important to never blame yourself and to tell an adult you trust as soon as possible.

- Not using alcohol and drugs will help you make clearer choices about sex. Too many young people have sex without meaning to when they drink alcohol or use drugs.

Are You Ready for Sex?

Sex can change your life and relationships. Having sex may affect the way you feel about yourself or how others feel about you.

Many teens believe waiting until they are ready to have sex is important. The right time is different for each teen. For example, some teens may want to wait until they are older (adults); other teens may want to wait until they feel their relationship is ready.

You may feel that your relationship is ready when:

- You can be completely honest and trust the other person, and the other person can trust you.

- You can talk with the person about difficult topics, such as feelings, other relationships, and if the person has had a sexually transmitted infection (STI).

- You can be responsible, protecting yourself and your partner against STIs and pregnancy with condoms and birth control.

- You can respect the other person's decisions about not having sex and about using protection.

However, if you are in love or like someone, you may ignore the signs of an unhealthy relationship.

The following signs mean your relationship is **not** ready for sex:

- Your partner is jealous or possessive. For example, your partner prevents you from spending time with your family or other friends, texts or instant messages you constantly, or checks your cell phone to see who you are talking with.

- Your partner pressures you to have sex and refuses to see your point of view.

- Your partner manipulates you by either bullying you or threatening to hurt himself if you end the relationship.

There's nothing wrong if you decide to wait. Not everyone is having sex. Half of all teens in the United States have never had sex. If you decide to wait, stick with your decision. Plan how you are going to say no, so you are clearly understood. Stay away from situations that can lead to sex.

Chapter 13:

Stop Setting Unrealistic Expectations of Your Partner

Are you wondering how to stop unmet expectations from ruining your relationship? Do you find yourself constantly disappointed with your partner and thinking about ending it?

There are ways to stop unmet expectations from ruining your relationship. Here are a few.

1. Identify Your Own

One way to stop unmet expectations from ruining your relationship is by questioning your own. What do you think you need from your partner? Do you need him to give up his friends and hobbies for you? Do you expect to have sex every night? Do you want her to keep the house spotlessly clean as your mother did? Do you expect him to anticipate your every need?

Expectations like these are exactly the things that can kill a relationship. I would encourage you to think about what you want from your partner so that it's clear in your mind. I also want you to consider if your expectations are reasonable.

If your expectations aren't reasonable, your relationship might be dead upon arrival. If you don't know your expectations, your partner will have a hard time reaching them because you might always be moving the goal post. So, before unmet expectations destroy your relationship, make sure you know what yours are.

2. Set Boundaries

I always encourage new couples to set boundaries in their relationships as soon as possible To understand healthy relationship boundaries, look at the four walls of your house. Those walls are the structure that holds your life together. They hold your food and your bed and your possessions, and it's where you live your life.

Healthy boundaries are the same as those four walls of your house. They are the things that support your relationship as it matures. To have a healthy relationship that can grow and be fruitful, it must have structures and boundaries that support it. Healthy boundaries come in many shapes, sizes, and colors.

A few examples:

- Make sure you stay yourself

- Allow yourselves time apart
- Communication is important
- Mutual respect at all times
- Keep the power dynamic equal
- Making time for both sides of the family
- Respecting others friends and hobbies

Of course, each couple needs to decide what works for them, but every couple must establish some boundaries early and stick to them for the sake of their relationship.

3. Be Truthful

You must discuss this with your partner if your expectations aren't being met. One of the most common complaints that I hear from women is 'he should know what I need. I shouldn't have to tell him.' And this, I am afraid, is mostly impossible. Men would love to anticipate and meet our needs, but many of them just don't always have it in them. This is not some deficiency of character but because men have no idea how women think and why. It's a mystery to them, so expecting them to be able to do so will set you up for disaster.

Chapter 14:

Why You Are Amazing

When was the last time you told yourself that you were amazing? Was it last week, last month, last year, or maybe not even once in your life?

As humans, we always seek to gain validation from our peers. We wait to see if something that we did recently warranted praise or commendation. Either from our colleagues, our bosses, our friends, or even our families. And when we don't receive those words that we expect them to, we think that we are unworthy, or that our work just wasn't good enough. That we are lousy and under serving of praise.

With social media and the power of the internet, these feelings have been amplified. For those of us that look at the likes on our Instagram posts or stories, or the number of followers on Tiktok, Facebook, or Snapchat, we allow ourselves to be subjected to the validation of external forces in order to qualify our self-worth. Whether these are strangers who don't know you at all, or whoever they might be, their approval seems to matter the most to us rather than the approval we can choose to give ourselves.

We believe that we always have to up our game in order to seek happiness. Everytime we don't get the likes, we let it affect our mood for the rest of the day or even the week.

Have you ever thought of how wonderful it is if you are your best cheerleader in life? If the only validation you needed to seek was from yourself? That you were proud of the work you put out there, even if the world disagrees, because you know that you have put your heart and soul into the project and that there was nothing else you could have done better in that moment when you were producing that thing?

I am here to tell you that you are amazing because only you have the power to choose to love yourself unconditionally. You have the power to tell yourself that you are amazing. and that you have the power to look into yourself and be proud of how far you came in life. To be amazed by the things that you have done up until this point, things that other people might not have seen, acknowledged, or given credit to you for. But you can give that credit to yourself. To pat yourself on the back and say "I did a great job".

I believe that we all have this ability to look inwards. That we don't need external forces to tell us we are amazing because deep down, we already know we are.

If nobody else in the world loves you, know that I do. I love your courage, your bravery, your resilience, your heart, your soul, your commitment, and your dedication to live out your best life on this earth. Tell yourself each and everyday that you deserve to be loved, and that you are loved.

Go through life fiercely knowing that you don't need to seek happiness, validations, and approval from others. That you have it inside you all along and that is all you need to keep going.

Chapter 15:

Understanding Yourself

Today we're going to talk about a topic that hopefully helps you become more aware of who you are as a person. And why do you exist right here and right now on this Earth. Because if we don't know who we are, if we don't understand ourselves, then how can we expect to other stand and relate to others? And why we even matter?

How many of you think that you can describe yourself accurately? If someone were to ask you exactly who you are, what would you say? Most of us would say we are Teachers, doctors, lawyers, etc. We would associate our lives with our profession.

But is that really what we are really all about?

Today I want to ask you not what you do, and not let your career define you, but rather what makes you feel truly alive and connected with the world? What is it about your profession that made you want to dedicated your life and time to it? Is there something about the job that makes you want to get up everyday and show up for the work, or is it merely to collect the paycheck at the end of the month?

I believe that that there is something in each and everyone of us that makes us who we are, and keeps us truly alive and full. For those that dedicate their lives to be Teachers, maybe they see themselves as an educator, a role model, a person who is in charge of helping a kid grow up, a nurturer, a parental figure. For Doctors, maybe they see themselves as healers, as someone who feels passionate about bringing life to someone. Whatever it may be, there is more to them than their careers.

For me, I see myself as a future caregiver, and to enrich the lives of my family members. That is something that I feel is one of my purpose in life. That I was born, not to provide for my family monetary per se, but to provide the care and support for them in their old age. That is one of my primary objectives. Otherwise, I see and understand myself as a person who loves to share knowledge with others, as I am doing right now. I love to help others in some way of form, either to inspire them, to lift their spirits, or to just be there for them when they need a crying shoulder. I love to help others fulfill their greatest potential, and it fills my heart with joy knowing that someone has benefitted from my advice. From what I have to say. And that what i have to say actually does hold some merit, some substance, and it is helping the lives of someone out there.. to help them make better decisions, and to help the, realise that life is truly wonderful. That is who i am.

Whenever I try to do something outside of that sphere, when what I do does not help someone in some way or another, I feel a sense of dread. I feel that what I do becomes misaligned with my calling, and I drag my feet each day to get those tasks done. That is something that I have realized about myself. And it might be happening to you too.

If u do not know exactly who you are and why you are here on this Earth, i highly encourage you to take the time to go on a self-discovery journey, however long it may take, to figure that out. Only when you know exactly who you are, can you start doing the work that aligns with ur purpose and calling. I don't meant this is in a religious way, but i believe that each and every one of us are here for a reason, whether it may to serve others, to help your fellow human beings, or to share your talents with the world, we should all be doing something with our lives that is at least close to that, if not exactly that.

So I challenge each and everyone of you to take this seriously because I believe you will be much happier for it. Start aligning your work with your purpose and you will find that life is truly worth living.

Chapter 16:

6 Signs You Are Emotionally Unavailable

In times of need, all we want is emotional comfort. The people around us mainly provide it. But the question is, will we support them if the need arises? You might be emotionally unavailable for them when they need you. It is necessary to have some emotional stability to form some strong bonds. If you are emotionally unapproachable, you will have fewer friends than someone you stand mentally tall. It is not harmful to be emotionally unavailable, but you need to change that in the long run. And for that, you need to reflect on yourself first.

It would help if you always were your top priority. While knowing why you are emotionally unapproachable, you need to focus on yourself calmly. Giving respect and talking is not enough for someone to rely on you. You need to support them whenever needed. Talk your mind with them. Be honest with them. But not in a rude way, in a comforting way. So, next time they will come to you for emotional support and comfort. If you are relating to all these things, then here are some signs that confirm it.

1.   You Keep People At A Distance

It is usual for an emotionally unavailable person to be seen alone at times. They tend to stay aloof at times; that way, they don't have to be emotionally available. And even if you meet people, you always find it challenging to make a bond with them. You might have a few friends and family members close to you. But you always find meeting new people an emotionally draining activity. You also might like to hang out with people, but opening up is not your forte. If you are emotionally unavailable, then you keep people at a hands distance from you.

2. You Have Insecurities

59

If you struggle to love yourself, then count it as a sign of emotional stress. People are likely to be unavailable emotionally for others when they are emotionally unavailable for themselves too. We always doubt the people who love us. How can they when I, myself, can't? And this self-hatred eventually results in a distant relationship with your fellow beings. Pampering yourself time by time is essential for every single one of us. It teaches us how one should be taken care of and how to support each other.

3. You Have A Terrible Past Experience

This could be one of the reasons for your unapproachable nature towards people. When you keep some terrible memory or trauma stored inside of you, it's most likely you cannot comfort some other being. It won't seem like something you would do. Because you keep this emotional difference, you become distant and are forced to live with those memories, making things worse. It would help if you talked things out. Either your parents or your friends. Tell them whatever is on your mind, and you will feel light at heart. Nothing can change the past once it's gone, but we can work on the future.

4. You Got Heartbroken

In most cases, people are not born with this nature to be emotionally unavailable. It often comes with heartbreak. If you had a breakup with your partner, that could affect your emotional life significantly. And if it was a long-term relationship, then you got emotionally deprived. But on the plus side, you got single again. Ready to choose from scratch. Instead, you look towards all the negative points of this breakup. Who knows, maybe you'll find someone better.

5. You Are An Introvert

Do you hate going to parties or gatherings? Does meeting with friends sound tiresome? If yes, then surprise, you are an introvert. Social life can be a mess sometimes. Sometimes we prefer a book to a person. That trait of ours makes us emotionally unavailable for others. It is not a bad thing to stay at home on a Friday night, but going out once in a while may be healthy for you. And the easiest way to do that is to make an extrovert friend. Then you won't need to make an effort. Everything will go smoothly.

6. You Hate Asking For Help

Do you feel so independent that you hate asking for help from others? Sometimes when we get support from others, we feel like they did a favor for us. So, instead of asking for help, we prefer to do everything alone, by ourselves. Asking for aid, from superior or inferior, is no big deal. Everyone needs help sometimes.

Conclusion

Being emotionally unavailable doesn't make you a wrong person, but being there for others gives us self-comfort too. It's not all bad to interact with others; instead, it's pretty fun if you try. It will make your life much easier, and you will have a lot of support too.

Chapter 17:

What Happens When You Get Bored In A Relationship

Being bored in your relationship can make you feel unpleasant emotions; you would not feel like yourself. You will be more likely to be over things that excited you before, like sex, date night, vacation with your partner, etc. Even if you don't feel like ending things, the lack of satisfaction would be enough to get you frustrated and ready to break up. Due to this boredom, you may feel stuck in a tedious cycle or feel suffocated. There are many things you will notice about yourself when you are bored of your relationship.

Picking unnecessary fights with your partner is one of the signs that you are bored with them. Dr. Binita Amin, a clinical psychologist, says getting into arguments for innocuous reasons might signify you are bored. If you find yourself bickering with your partner for petty reasons, then you may want to step back and assess why. Boredom can efficiently fuel arguments, but disagreements happen in any relationship; the best way is to see if these arguments are indeed caused by boredom.

Your frustration with your relationship causes these arguments. You can always figure out what is exactly causing this boredom, and maybe you can overcome this problem and carry out a healthy relationship.

Sometimes, we all enjoy comfortable silence, but is that silence comfortable anymore, or is it just because you have no more to speak to each other. Silent meals even when you are in a sit-in restaurant, or even if a few words are exchanged, but those words are in safe and predictable confines, then that is a sign that you are bored. To prevent this, you can try strengthening your bond with your partner.

When we first meet a person we like or at the beginning of a relationship, we put our best self forward, we try to be perfect for them, but when a person feels bored, they no longer place any effort into their relationship. They don't bother looking nice for a date night or don't bother waiting for them at the dinner table because we all know such factors lead to a healthy relationship. Being bored in a relationship can lead to an unhealthy period of your life. But if you are putting in the effort, you know that boredom is far away from your relationship and you.

Have you ever wondered about what it would be like to be with someone else? Even when you are in a relationship. If you have, then that is a sign that you have fallen victim to boredom. It is natural for a person to find more than one person attractive but always pay attention to what is the factor that is causing you to daydream about someone else, and it is simply because you are bored with your relationship. Because if that is the case, you need to make your relationship more exciting or talk and discuss matters with your partner.

Many people in this world are happy to be single, as they say, to be free of any commitment but are that the case with you. Do you wish that you were single? Or envying the single status of your friends? If yes, then you need to take a closer look at your relationship; it may turn out that you feel bored with your relationship, that you no longer feel the passion and excitement of the earlier days of your relationship. If you are glad that your partner is busy with something else, then that is a sign that you are bored.

Don't let boredom be the end of your relationship; you can seek help from relationship counselors, or you can sit around and discuss these matters. Together you can always find a solution to every problem. All relationship requires efforts, so put in your step and let your relationship bloom.

Chapter 18:

Things That Spark Joy

I'm sure you've heard the term "spark joy", and this is our topic of discussion today that I am going to borrow heavily from Marie Kondo.

Now why do I find the term spark joy so fascinating and why have i used it extensively in all areas of my life ever since coming across that term a few years ago?

When I first watched Marie Kondo's show on Netflix and also reading articles on how this simple concept that she has created has helped people declutter their homes by choosing the items that bring joy to them and discarding or giving away the ones that don't, I began my own process of decluttering my house of junk from clothes to props to ornaments, and even to furniture.

I realised that many things that looked good or are the most aesthetically pleasing, aren't always the most comfortable to use or wear. And when they are not my go to choice, they tend to sit on shelves collecting dust and taking up precious space in my house. And after going through my things one by one, this recurring theme kept propping up time and again. And i subconsciously associated comfort and ease of use with things that spark joy to me. If I could pick something up easily without hesitation to use or wear, they tend to me things that I gravitated to naturally, and these things began to spark joy when i used them. And when i started getting rid of things that I don't find particularly pleased to use, i felt my house was only filled with enjoyable things that I not only enjoyed looking at, but also using on a regular and frequent basis.

This association of comfort and ease of use became my life philosophy. It didn't apply to simply just decluttering my home, but also applied to the process of acquiring in the form of shopping. Every time i would pick something up and consider if it was worthy of a purpose, i would examine whether this thing would be something that I felt was comfortable and that i could see myself utilising, and if that answer was no, i would put them down and never consider them again because i knew deep down that it would not spark joy in me as I have associated joy with comfort.

This simple philosophy has helped saved me thousands of dollars in frivolous spending that was a trademark of my old self. I would buy things on the fly without much consideration and most often they would end up as white elephants in my closet or cupboard.

To me, things that spark joy can apply to work, friends, and relationships as well. Expanding on the act of decluttering put forth by Marie Kondo. If the things you do, and the people you hang out with don't spark you much joy, then why bother? You would be better off spending time doing things with people that you actually find fun and not waste everybody's time in the process. I believe you would also come out of it being a much happier person rather than forcing yourself to be around people and situations that bring you grief.

Now that is not to say that you shouldn't challenge yourself and put yourself out there. But rather it is to give you a chance to assess the things you do around you and to train yourself to do things that really spark joy in you that it becomes second nature. It is like being fine tuned to your 6th sense in a way because ultimately we all know what we truly like and dislike, however we choose to ignore these feelings and that costs us time effort and money.

So today's challenge is for you to take a look at your life, your home, your friendships, career, and your relationships. Ask yourself, does this thing spark joy? If it doesn't, maybe you should consider a decluttering of sorts from all these different areas in your life and to streamline it to a more minimalist one that you can be proud of owning each and every piece.

Take care and I'll see you in the next one.

Chapter 19:

Fight Is The Reward

There are times in our lives when we feel blocked out. When we feel the darkness coming in. When we see the sun going down and seemingly never coming back up. When the winds feel tougher and everything coming in your way puts you down like a storm.

No matter how big and how defiant you get, life will always find a new way to knock you down.

You will often find yourself in a place where you have nowhere to go, but straight. And that straight path isn't always the easiest too. It has all these ridges and peaks or a long ditch. So you finally come to realize that the only way out is a challenge itself and you can't bow out because there is no other way around.

I want you to understand the concept of fight and struggle. The success stories and breakthroughs we all hear are mostly just 2 parts; its 90% work and 10% fight.

We all work and we all work hard. But the defining moment of our journey is the final fight we go through.

The work we put in gets us to the bottom of the final barrier but the effort we need to summit the peak is the fight we put in and finally get the breakthrough. But fighting isn't easy. It is the hardest part of your journey to success.

The fight you need to put in isn't just the Xs and O's. The true fight is your mental toughness. It's your sheer will to keep going and keep pushing because you are just around the corner for the ultimate success.

You are just on the verge of finding the best reward of your life. You are on the cusp of seeing and enjoying your happiest moments. Because you have finally found your dreams and you have finally fulfilled your purpose in life.

Now is the time to rise and give up the feeling of giving up. Now is the time to get on top of your challenges. Now is the time to sweat and get over that pain.

This is the moment you need to be at your best. This is the time you need your A-game. This is the time to defy all odds and go all in. Because the finals moments need the final straw of strength and effort in your body.

Make a decision and become your own light. Believe in yourself like you have never before and you will never look back.

So if you ask me again why is fighting worth it. It's because your attitude makes you win long before you have even set the foot in the battleground. It's your will to keep going that makes you stand out even before getting into the spotlight.

You don't win a fight when you fight, you win a fight before the fight even begins. Your ultimate reward is the collection of all your efforts and resilience.

Chapter 20:

<u>Take Ownership of Yourself</u>

What belongs to you but is used by other people more than you?
Your name.

And that's okay. People can use your name. But you must never allow yourself to lose ownership of you. In fact, you need to be incredibly conscious of taking ownership of everything that you are. And I do mean everything. Those few extra pounds, the nose you think is too big, your ginger hair or freckled skin. Whatever it is that you are insecure about, it's time that you showed up and took ownership. Because the moment you do your world will change.

But what does that look like? Why does it matter?

If someone parks a limo in the road outside your house, hands you the keys and tells you it is yours, what would you do? You're not just gonna put the keys in the ignition and leave it in the road. You are going to put that thing in a garage and get it insured. You will make sure that it is in a place where it is safe from weather and your jealous neighbour. Those are the things that you do when you take ownership of something. You make sure that they are protected because you value them. Then when you drive around town you don't look around as if you've stolen the thing. You drive with style and confidence. You are bold and comfortable because it belongs to you. *That* is what ownership looks like.

Now I know what you're thinking. That's easy to do with a limo, but I what I have is the equivalent of a car built before world war two. But the beautiful thing about ownership is that it does not depend on the object. It is not the thing being owned that you have to worry about, all you have to do is claim it. You've seen teenagers when they get their first car. Even if it is an old rust-bucket they drive around beaming with pride. Why? Because they know that what they have is theirs. It belongs to them and so they take ownership of it.

You have to do the same. You must take ownership of every part of you because in doing so you will keep it secure. You no longer have to be insecure about your weight if you know that that is where you are at right now. That doesn't mean you don't work for change though. It doesn't give you an excuse for stagnancy. You take accountability for your change and growth as much as you do for your present state. But in taking ownership you work towards polishing your pride, not getting rid of your low self-esteem. The difference may sound semantic, but the implications are enormous. The one allows you to work towards something and get somewhere good. The other makes it feel like you are just running away from something. And when you are running away then the only direction that matters is away – even if that means you run in circles.

Make a change today. Own yourself once more and be amazed at the rush that comes with it. With ownership comes confidence.

Chapter 21:

Discovering Your Purpose

If you guys don't already know, this is one of the topics that I really love talking about. And I never get tired of it. Having a purpose is something that I always believe everyone should have. Having a purpose to live, to breathe, to get up each day, I believe that without purpose, there is no point to life.

So today we're going to talk about how to discover your purpose, and why you should make it a point to find one if you didn't already start looking.

So what is purpose exactly. A purpose is a reason to do something. Is to have something else greater than ourselves to work for. You see, I believe if we are only focused on ourselves, instead of others, we will not be able to be truly happy in life. Feeding our own self interests does not bring us joy as one might think. After living the life that I had, I realized that true happiness only comes when you bring joy to someone else's life. Whether it be helping others professionally or out of selflessness, this happiness will radiate and reflect back to us from someone else who is appreciative of your efforts.

On some level, we can look into ourselves to be happy. For example being grateful for life, loving ourselves, and all that good stuff. Yes keep doing those things. But there is a whole other dimension if we devote our time and energy into helping others once we have already conquered ourselves. If you look at many of the most successful people on the planet, after they have acquired an immense amount of wealth, many of them look to passion projects or even philanthropy where they can give back to the community when having more money doesn't do anything for them anymore. If you look at Elon Musk and Jeff Bezos, these two have a greater purpose which is their space projects. Where they visualise humans being able to move out of Earth one day where civilisation is able to expand. Or Bill Gates and Warren Buffet, who have pledged to give billions of their money away for philanthropic work, to help the less fortunate and to fund organisations that work towards finding cures to diseases.

Now for us mere mortals, we don't need to think so big. Our purpose need not be so extravagant. It can be as simple as having a purpose to provide for your loved one, to work hard to bring your family members of holidays and travel, or to bring joy to your elderly relatives by organising activities for them to do. There is no purpose that is too big or too small.

Your purpose could be helping others find a beautiful home, doing charitable work, or even feeding and providing for your growing family.

As humans, we will automatically work harder if we have a clear and defined purpose. We have a reason to get up each day, to go to work, to earn that paycheck, so that we can spend it on things and people, even ourselves at times. Without a purpose, we struggle to find meaning in the work that we do. We struggle to see the big picture and we find that we have no reason to work so hard, or even at all. And we struggle to find life worth living.

This revelation came to me when I started seeing my work as helping some other person in a meaningful way. Where my work was not just about making money to buy nice things, but to be able to impact someone else's life in a positive way. That became my purpose. To see them learn something new, and to bring a joy and smile to their faces. That thought that I was contributing something useful to someone made me smile more than money ever could. Yes money can help you live a comfortable life, but helping others can go a much farther way into giving your life true purpose.

So I challenge each and everyone of you to find a purpose in everything that you do, and if you struggle to find one, start by making the goal to help others a priority. Think of the difference you can make to others and that could very well be your purpose in life as well.

I believe in each and every one of you.. I hope you learned something today and as always, take care and I'll see you in the next one.

Chapter 22:

10 Facts About Attraction

Everything from taking an interest in someone to admire someone physically or mentally is known as an attraction. The attraction could be a romantic or sexual feeling. Attraction can be confusing and takes time to understand. Most of us find it hard to know what we feel about or are attracted to someone. We couldn't figure out what type of attraction it is, but we should remember there is no right way to feel the attraction. There are so many types of attraction, and some could happen at once.

1. **Women attracted to older men:**

So, it is expected that most women these days are attracted to older men just because of their "daddy issues" and the most one is the financial issue but according to study it's not the reason. According to authentic references or studies, the women born to old fathers are attracted to older men, and the women born to younger men are attracted to younger men. As they think that they will treat them just like their father did.

2. **Opposite attraction:**

As we all heard before, "opposite attracts." well, it is true, according to a study of the university of dresden, that both men and women are attracted to different leukocyte antigens, which is also known as the hla complex. A genetic blueprint responsible for the immune function is so unique that this attraction has to do with species' survival. Now, how do our brains detect the opposite hla complex? According to a study, our brain can see the opposite hla complex only by the scents; isn't it a fascinating fact?

3. The tone of women's voices:

According to a study by the university of canada, when women flirt, their voice pitch increases automatically. Not only while flirting, but women's voice tones increase at different emotions. The highest tone of a woman's voice gets when she is fertile or ovulated, and guess what? According to studies, men like the most high-pitched voices of women.

4. Whisper in the left ear:

According to a study, when you want to intimate someone, like whispering " i love you" in their ear, then whisper in their left ear because whispering in the left ear has 6% more effect than a whisper in the right one.

5. Red dress:

Red dress attracts both men and women. It is examined in a study that usually men love women in the red dress. They find it intimidating.

6. Men with beard:

Women find men attractive with a beard. Beard with the subtle cut. Another fantastic fact about the beard is that women judged men with a beard to be a better choice for a long-term relationship. This might be because men with beards look more mature and responsible. Beard also makes you look like you have a higher status in society.

7. Men trying to sound sexy:

So, women have no trouble whatsoever changing their voice, but men have no clue about it. Women lower their voice pitch and make it sexy, and men find it so attractive, but men find it very difficult to sound sexy. It got a little bit worse when men tried to say sexy. The reason behind this is elaborated in research, according to which men are not focused on making their voice sexy but women do.

8. Competing:

Research shows that when you are famous for everyone, and everyone likes them, you get attracted to them and try to get them. You start competing for that person with other people, which makes you feel more attracted to that person. That person will be in your head all the time because you see everyone admiring and chasing that person.

9. **Adrenaline:**

Studies show that adrenaline has to do a lot with attraction. People find others more attractive when they are on an adrenaline rush themselves. According to a study, women find men more attractive when they are ovulating than in another period.

10. **Weights and heights:**

When taking a liking to someone. People always prefer to choose a person who holds the right weight and height according to them. Different people may have different opinions. When they find a person with a likable body, they get easily attracted to them.

Conclusion:

Attraction to someone can play a significant role in getting them. When people are attracted to you, they make you feel worth it all, and you feel ecstatic. Attraction can be=ring in a lot of factors like popularity, relationship and of course, love.

Chapter 23:
When To Listen To That Voice Inside Your Head

Everyday we hear a voice in our head telling us things to us. Whether it be a negative voice telling us not to do something, or a positive one that pushes us to try something new, we sometimes forget when and when not to listen to it.

Today I found myself in that very situation. I found myself walking going about my day when I heard a voice telling me that I should go back to my passion, which was to record music, and simply used my voice as the only tool to make music. I had heard this voice many times before, but i always brushed it away because I thought to myself, no one is going to want to hear me sing. Why should anyone? My voice sucks. It's not as good as other people. No one is going to like it. And I am just going to waste my time. Those negative voices always found a way to beat down my positive one to the point where I just gave up listening to them altogether because I figured that I was never going to act on anything out of my fears to do so anyway.

But something happened today that made me listen. Today I felt like it had a point to make and it was trying to get out. and today those goblin voices that usually tried to kill that positive one was silent. I took that opportunity to head straight down to the nearest electronics store, to buy an expensive mic, and decided that I was going to pursue this venture no matter what. I wanted to do it for myself. I wanted to do it because I didn't want to regret not listening to that inner voice 10-20-30 years down the road. Sure people might still not listen to me sing, but dammit i was going to do it anyway.

It didn't matter to me if only 5 people liked it. It mattered more that I liked it. It mattered more that I overcame myself and finally put music out there that I was proud of.

I bought that mic because I didn't want the excuses in my head to start creeping up on me again. I bought that mic because it gave me no way out. I was already committed. And if I didn't do it I would've just wasted a ton of money. Sometimes in life you have to push yourself and give no reasons to turn back. Because it is always easy just to give up. But when that object is staring at you, sitting and calling out to you, you are going to one to use it.

We all have voices in our heads that tell us to do something crazy but magical in our lives. We shove them aside because we are afraid. We shove them aside because we don't dare to dream. We shove them aside because we think we are not good enough. We fail to realize that we are just one decision away from changing our lives.

Carrie Underwood, for those of you who don't know who she is, she won American Idol in 2005 and became one of the biggest country music superstars in the world. Did you know that she almost didn't make the trip to audition for American Idol because that goblin voice in her head told her it was a stupid idea to go? In that split second decision where she decided to try anyway, it changed her life forever. She changed the music scene forever. It was crazy to think a girl from a small town could win as many Grammys as she did, but she did.

This is the same dilemma you and I face everyday. We fail to realize that everytime we say no to that crazy idea, we are taking one step back in our lives. Soon we become so used to taking these steps back that we end up taking them forever, failing to achieve anything great in the process. Life is simply one giant list of decisions that we make on a daily basis. Any decision that we choose not to take, is a decision that is either missed, or lost.

Start listening to what that voice inside your head has been telling you to do. Has there been something that has been painfully obvious to you? A voice that has been recurring that you've been shoving aside? Take a pen, write that voice down on apiece of paper. Dig into it and start finding out if you should be taking action on it. You never know what that one decision can do for the rest of your life unless you give it a shot.

Chapter 24:

Discovering Your Strengths and Weaknesses

Today we're going to talk about a very simple yet important topic that hopefully brings about some self discovery about who you really are. By the end of this video i wish to help you find out what areas you are weak at so that maybe you could work on those, and what your strengths are so that you can play to them and lean into them more for greater results in your career and life in general.

We should all learn to accept our flaws as much as we embrace our strengths. And we have to remember that each of us are unique and we excel in different areas. Some of us are more artistic, some visionary, some analytical, some hardworking, some lazy, what matters is that we make these qualities work for us in our own special way.

Let's start by identifying your weaknesses. For those of you that have watched enough of my videos, you would know that i encourage all of you to take a pen to write things down. So lets go through this exercise real quick. Think of a few things that people have told you that you needed to work on, be it from your Teachers, your friends, your family, or whoever it may be.

How many of these weaknesses would you rate as significantly important that it would affect your life in a drastic way if you did not rectify it? I want you to put them at the top of your list. Next spend some time to reflect and look in the mirror. Be honest with yourself and identify the areas about yourself that you know needs some work.

Now I want you to take some time to identity your strengths. Repeat the process from above, what are the things people have told you about yourself that highlighted certain qualities about you? Whether that you're very outgoing, friendly, a great singer, a good team player, very diligent. I want you to write as many of these down as you can. No matter how big or small these strengths are, I want you to write down as many as you can.

Now I want you to also place your 3 biggest strengths at the top of the list. As I believe these are the qualities that best represent who you are as a person.

Now that you've got these 2 lists. I want you to compare them. Which list is longer? the one with strengths or weaknesses? If you have more weaknesses, that's okay, it just means that there is more room for improvement. If you have more strengths, thats good.

What we are going to do with this list now is to now make it a mission to improve our weaknesses and play heavily into our strengths for the foreseeable future. You see, our strengths are strengths for a reason, we are simply naturally good at it. Whether it be through genetics, or our personalities, or the way we have been influenced by the world. We should all try to showcase our strengths as much as we can. It is hard for me to say exactly what that is, but I believe that you will know how you maximise the use of your talent. Whether it be serving others, performing for others, or even doing specific focused tasks. Simply do more of it. Put yourself in more situations where you can practice these strengths. And keep building on it. It will take little effort but yield tremendous results.

As for your weaknesses, I want you to spend some time on the top 3 that you have listed so far. As these could be the areas that have been holding you back the most. Making improvements in these areas could be the breakthrough that you need to become a much better person and could see you achieving a greater level success than if you had just left them alone.

I challenge each and everyone of you to continually play to your strengths, sharpening them until they are sharp as a knife, while working on smoothening the rough edges of your weaknesses. So that they may balance out your best qualities.

I hope that you have learned something today. Keep working on yourself and I believe in each and every one of you. Take care and I'll see you in the next one.

Chapter 25:

10 Ways To Build A Strong Relationship

Relationships are not always easy, especially when both people aren't exactly on the same page. But the key to a strong and healthy relationship doesn't necessarily mean you guys are mirror images of each other when it comes to your opinions and personality. Understanding and adaptability is the key to a successful relationship.

When it comes down to the two people involved, no two relationships are the same. As we are unique individuals, so will our relationships be as well. The needs, goals, perceptions, and growth vary from couple to couple. With that in mind, we are going to talk about the 10 signs that point to a strong relationship that all couples should strive for at some point in their time together.

1.Trust.

The foundation of any relationship is very much dependent on trust. More than love, trust is more important for the bond to be strong. Trust includes honesty, integrity, and at the same time feeling safe and comfortable with the person that you are with.

Trust has to be earned over time, by proving to your partner that they can count on you to be faithful in the relationship and also to be honest with things that are going on with your life.

Trust is also earned when you work with your partner in the same domain and you have a clear understanding of their passions.

2. Respect for personal space.

I feel that this needs to be heard loud and clear. Being in a relationship does not imply breathing down the neck of your partner all the time.

Doing so could potentially suffocate the other person and make the relationship bitter over time.

I am sure you don't like your personal space to be violated by someone else all the time, so expect the same adverse reactions if you do that to your partner as well.

It is very important that each individual in the relationship has the utmost respect for the other person's private space. Allowing room to breathe can be a wonderful way to recharge and come back to the relationship with renewed excitement and interest.

3. Spending quality time with your partner.

It is very important for two people in a relationship to spend quality time together. A certain time each week that you have set aside for your partner where the two of you will focus only on each other and nothing else. A time when you ask your partner the deep questions, to engage in insightful thought, or to simply be mindfully present in each other's company. It is an amazing feeling when your significant other engages you by asking about your day, asking how you are feeling, and making sure you are well taken care of.

While many thinks that quantity of time is important as well, I would argue that this could lead to complacency. It is important that you don't treat spending time with your partner by counting the hours, but by counting the moments instead.

4. Encouraging each other to achieve personal goals.

When your partner becomes your life coach who motivates you to become a better person every day and achieve your personal goals , this is where the bond grows beyond the surface level feelings into a much deeper emotional and spiritual connection.

By understanding the kind of service you need to provide to your partner to support their goals and dreams, you are in effect helping them achieve what they truly want in life. This proactiveness will make them fall in love with themselves and with you even more.

5. Physical Intimacy.

Physical intimacy doesn't necessarily imply sex. Sex is not necessary for a relationship to stick on provided both sides are on the same page. Even cuddles, hugs, and kissing your partner is an act of intimacy that is very important in any relationship. It is very crucial to have that understanding in the bedroom and to be able to openly express your needs, your desires, and your fantasies, and your inhibitions regarding physical intimacy with your partner. Lack of physical touch could result in loss of intimacy away from the bedroom. So be mindful that you keep that in check in your relationship.

6. Communication.

There is nothing more important than keeping the communication flowing with your partner. If you aren't comfortable in sharing your deepest emotions, fears, and insecurities with that person, you should probably think about why that is so. Your better half should not just be your partner in a relationship but should ideally by a very close and personal friend as well. There should not be inhibitions about expressing one's feelings and opinions about a matter out of fear that it might end up in a fight with the other person. Fights will inevitably happen in every relationship. How you manage the fights is what makes or breaks your strong bond.

7. Teamwork.

A relationship would become a burden if one person is constantly working hard to keep the other person comfortable and the other one doesn't contribute much. As the saying goes, team work makes the dream work. Be it household chores, cleaning the dishes, settling the bills, taking the dog out for a dump, both have to contribute equally for it to be a balanced relationship. Both will need to take the initiative to help out the other party where possible otherwise resentment and unhappiness might follow.

8. Personal Time.

This point overlaps quite a bit with providing personal space. To be a more balanced individual, you really need to have that "me-time" for yourself. Time where you spend alone. Time where you engage in your favourite hobbies or sports that you might not share with your partner.

Giving yourself that "me-time" can also include having that favorite cup of coffee while watching your favorite shows, catching up with your friends, cooking your favorite meal, or watching your favorite team match. Once you start balancing time for yourself you start respecting your partner's personal space and time as well, and that gives the relationship a breath of fresh air and keeps you both going.

9. Talking to your partner, not to other people.

It is very easy in times of fights to simply run away from the problems you are facing and into your friends for shelter. While having a strong social support network is great to have, always ensure that you come back to the relationship with a clear mind and talk things through openly and without fear of judgement.

Miscommunications are usually high up on the list when it comes to disagreements. It is always best to sort out the differences there instead of running away and letting the situation escalate to an unresolvable point.

10. The 3 golden phrases.

Yes, you are right. In a relationship, you should be able to say 'I am sorry', 'Thank you', and 'I love you' as much as possible. Being able to express your love, regret, appreciativeness, and sorrow, will enlighten the bond between you and your partner. By verbally saying these words regularly, you are showing your partner that you can be vulnerable around them and that they can be the same with you.

A Strong relationship is not easy to build, but it is worth the effort if we take the time and effort to put into practice some of these points that we have discussed today. Take care and I'll see you in the next one.

Chapter 26:

9 New Date Ideas That Will Deepen Your Relationship

When you commit to a relationship, you need to know your partner well. If you don't know your partner, then how do you expect your relationship to last? A date is something that someone plans for their partner. Dates usually involve doing something or going somewhere with your partner, and you find it fun, but sometimes everybody gets bored of the same cliché date ideas. Sometimes, these kinds of dates aren't enough to know your partner. Surely you want to deepen your bond with your partner. Here are some new date ideas to deepen your relationship.

1. Go For A Walk

We have often seen people go for a walk to clear their minds. Walking helps people think differently. It is not exactly an epic date idea, but it will remove both of your brains. It'll help you talk to each other. When you and your partner start talking more, your bond will automatically deepen. After the walk, you will feel very fresh, but you will also feel like you now know your partner more.

2. Read A Book Together

As a kid, we all loved to hear some bedtime stories, but we forgot how blissful it felt as we grew up. At night when both of you feel tired, then select a book you both like, lay down and read it to each other in turns.

3. Spa At Home

We all need some time to relax. You don't always have to go outside for a date, and you could give yourself a day off and bring out all the face, hair, and every other mask you have because this is a spa day, you could give each other massages and help the other relax. Also, don't forget the scented candles.

4. Plan Trips Together

Haven't we all dreamed about discovering the world but don't tell anyone, well what are you waiting for? Sit together and look through places you would want to visit even if you can't right now! Daydreaming isn't a sin.

5. Go For A Boat Ride

Have you watched tangled? If yes, you would surely want to experience that romantic scene on the boat; if you haven't still done it, what are you waiting for? Rent a boat, take your partner with you. It'll just be you, your partner, and the stars. You could set some slow music on your phone and enjoy that quality time with your partner.

6. Take A Step Out Of Your Comfort Zone

Almost all of us have a fixed routine, but it is good to mess with your way once in a while. As a couple, you would have a place where you usually go for food, a cinema where you typically watch a movie, an ice cream parlor where you usually buy the ice cream from but isn't it all getting boring? This is the time to forget about your comfort zone and explore something else. Go to a new restaurant, a museum you haven't been to before together, or any other place you and your partner haven't visited yet.

7. **Paint Together**

Not all of us are good at painting, but what's stopping you from painting something together. It sounds fun, doesn't it? Just buy a few art supplies and a canvas and paint whatever you want to paint. Then hang it somewhere; it seems nice, it doesn't need to be an artistic masterpiece, but it'll bring back the memories of that fantastic day whenever you look at it.

8. **Watch The Sunset Together**

There are many places where you can see the sunset together, so find the home that feels perfect to you and take your partner there for a date and watch the sunset together along with your partner's favorite dish to eat. Not only will this bring a wide smile to your partner's face, but it'll also help you deepen your connection with them.

9. **Meet At A Coffee Shop**

At the start of a relationship, most people decide to meet at a coffee shop, but as time passes, they don't do it anymore, but why not? Decide a time and a coffee shop and meet up there. Drink coffee and eat something if you like. You will have fun with this typical date idea.

Conclusion:

These simple and fun ideas will help you deepen your relationship with your partner. Don't fret if you think you don't know your partner much because it is never too late. Just put in some effort, and your bond with your partner would be more profound than the ocean.

Chapter 27:

6 Ways To Attract Anything You Want In Life

It is common human nature that one wants whatever one desires in life. People work their ways to get what they need or want. This manifestation of wanting to attract things is almost in every person around us. A human should be determined to work towards his goal or dreams through sheer hard work and will. You have to work towards it step by step because no matter what we try or do, we will always have to work for it in the end. So, it is imperative to work towards your goal and accept the fact that you can't achieve it without patience and dedication.

We have to start by improving ourselves day by day. A slight change a day can help us make a more considerable change for the future. We should feel the need to make ourselves better in every aspect. If we stay the way we are, tomorrow, we will be scared of even a minor change. We feel scared to let go of our comfort zone and laziness. That way, either we or our body can adapt to the changes that make you better, that makes you attract better.

1. Start With Yourself First

We all know that every person is responsible for his own life. That is why people try to make everything revolves around them. It's no secret that everyone wants to associate with successful, healthy, and charming people. But, what about ourselves? We should also work on ourselves to become the person others would admire. That is the type of person people love. He can also easily attract positive things to himself. It becomes easier to be content with your desires. We need to get ourselves together and let go of all the things we wouldn't like others doing.

2. Have A Clear Idea of Your Wants

Keeping in mind our goal is an easy way to attract it. Keep reminding yourself of all the pending achievements and all the dreams. It helps you work towards it, and it enables you to attract whatever you want. Make sure that you are aware of your intentions and make them count in your lives. You should always make sure to have a crystal-clear idea of your mindset, so you will automatically work towards it. It's the most basic principle to start attracting things to you.

3. Satisfaction With Your Achievements

It is hard to stop wanting what you once desired with your heart, but you should always be satisfied with anything you are getting. This way, when you attract more, you become happier. So, it is one of the steps to draw things, be thankful. Be thankful for what you are getting and what you haven't. Every action has a reason for itself. It doesn't mean just to let it be. Work for your goals but also acknowledge the ones already achieved by you in life. That way you will always be happy and satisfied.

4. Remove Limitations and Obstacles

We often limit ourselves during work. We have to know that there is no limit to working for what you want when it comes to working for what you want. You remove the obstacles that are climbing their way to your path. It doesn't mean to overdo yourselves, but only to check your capability. That is how much pressure you can handle and how far you can go in one go. If you put your boundaries overwork, you will always do the same amount, thus, never improving further. Push yourself a little more each time you work for the things you want in life.

5. Make Your Actions Count

We all know that visualizing whatever you want makes it easier to get. But we still cannot ignore the fact that it will not reach us unless we do some hard work and action. Our actions speak louder than words, and they speak louder than our thoughts. So, we have to make sure that our actions are built of our brain image. That is the way you could attract the things you want in life. Action is an essential rule for attracting anything you want in life.

6. Be Optimistic About Yourselves

Positivity is an essential factor when it comes to working towards your goals or dreams. When you learn to be optimistic about almost everything, you will notice that everything will make you satisfied. You will attract positive things and people. Negative vibes will leave you disappointed in yourself and everyone around you. So, you will have to practice positivity. It may not be easy at first while everyone around you is pushing you to negativity. That is where your test begins, and you have to prove yourself to them and yourself. And before you know it, you are attracting things you want.

Conclusion

Everyone around us wants to attract what they desire, but you have to start with yourself first. You only have to focus on yourself to achieve what you want. And attracting things will come naturally to you. Make sure you work for your dreams and goals with all your dedication and determination. With these few elements, you will be attracting anything you want.

Chapter 28:

6 Ways To Be More Confident In Bed

Confidence is something a lot of people inherit naturally, while others could work on. When you're confident and comfortable in your skin, people assume that you have a reason to be, and then they react and respect you accordingly. You can be confident all you want at work or on dates, but what about being confident in bed? Being confident sexually can be enjoyable for both you and your partner. It isn't just at ease sexual, but also it's comfortable with the way you express and experience your sexuality.

Sexual confidence can be measured by how authentically you can relate intimately either with yourself or your partner and how pure and vulnerable you are in that sexual space where you feel like giving your 100 percent to be yourself and communicate the pleasure you desire. Building your confidence in bed can crucially improve your sex life. Here are some tips on how to be more confident in bed.

1. Do What You're Already Confident In

Even if you are insecure and think you lack sexual skills, there must be at least a tiny thing that you might be good at. Maybe you don't feel confident enough about your kissing skills, but you're a great cuddler, or perhaps you feel shaky about touching and teasing but are good vocally.

Focus on what you're good at and polish that skill every time you're in bed with your partner. This will help you boost your confidence and might even convince you to try something new with them.

2. Try Something New

Once you start considering yourself as the master of that one skill you have been practicing, you would end up craving to try new things. Start with the things you're less comfortable with; maybe stepping out of your comfort zone might be enjoyable for you after all. You neither have to perfect the skill nor be a master of it, just trying it out can be fun in itself. It might be helpful to broaden the sexual script so that it doesn't look the same every time and bore your partner, but instead, trying new things can be an excellent adventure for you as well as your partner.

3. Laugh It Off If You Trip Up

You can't be good at everything you try in bed, nor should you be. What matters is how well you keep your attitude, and if you can have fun with it and have a great laugh if things go south, that's an achievement in itself. If you have already built up consistent self-confidence, then you can laugh it out loud on something that you can't get a grip on. After all, there might always be some things you'll be bad at and others in which you'll be a master.

4. Focus On What You Love About Your Body

There are instances where we will be utterly insecure about our bodies and features. There are some physical traits that we don't like but have made peace with, while others that we want but don't appreciate enough. The next time you look in the mirror, focus more on what you like about your face and body, be confident in them, and the things you don't like about yourself will vanish automatically.

5. Wear What Makes You Feel Confident

There is no particular stuff you have to wear or the way you have to look to feel more confident, but if you wear a look that you think looks great, you must go with it. Chances are, you will start feeling better about yourself instantly. If you feel more confident wearing lipstick, then wear it to bed, or if you think sexier wearing a lotion, use it before bed. Do whatever makes you feel like a total hottie.

6. Repeat A Mantra

We have all heard of the phrase "fake it till you make it." So, there's no harm in faking affirmations till you start believing in them. Keep repeating "I'm confident, I've got this" till it gets through. Affirmations increase how positively we feel about ourselves.

Conclusion

The task of becoming confident may seem daunting, but these small sub-tasks are an easy way to start. Another plus point is once you have practiced these techniques in bed, the confidence will spill over into every area of your life.

Chapter 29:

6 Signs You Have A Fear of Intimacy

Intimacy avoidance or avoidance anxiety, also sometimes referred to as the fear of intimacy, is characterized as the fear of sharing a close emotional or physical relationship with someone. People who experience it do not consciously want to avoid intimacy; they even long for closeness, but they frequently push others away and may even sabotage relationships for many reasons.

The fear of intimacy is separate from the fear of vulnerability, though both of them can be closely intertwined. A person who has a fear of intimacy may be comfortable becoming vulnerable and showing their true self to their trusted friends and relatives. This problem often begins when a person finds relationships becoming too close or intimate. Fear of intimacy can stem from several causes. Overcoming this fear and anxiety can take time, but you can work on it if you know the signs of why you have the fear in the first place.

1. Fear Of Commitment

A person who has a fear of intimacy can interact well with others initially. It's when the relationship and its value grow closer that everything starts to fall apart. Instead of connecting with your partner on an intimate level, you find ways and excuses to end the relationship and replace it with yet another superficial relationship. Some might even call you a 'serial dater,' as you tend to lose interest after a few dates and abruptly end the relationship. The pattern of emerging short-term relationships and having a 'commitment phobia' can signify that you fear intimacy.

2. Perfectionism

The idea of erfectionism often works to push others away rather than draw them near. The underlying fear of intimacy often lies in a person who thinks he does not deserve to be loved and supported. The constant need for someone to prove themself to be perfect and lovable can cause people to drift apart from them. Absolute perfectionism lies in being imperfect. We should be able to accept the flaws of others and should expect them to do the same for us. There's no beauty in trying to be perfect when we know we cannot achieve it.

3. Difficulty Expressing Needs

A person who has a fear of intimacy may have significant difficulty in expressing needs and wishes. This may stem from feeling undeserving of another's support. You need to understand that people cannot simply 'mind read,' they cannot know your needs by just looking at you; this might cause you to think that your needs go unfulfilled and your feelings of unworthiness are confirmed. This can lead to a vicious cycle of you not being vocal about your needs and lacking trust in your partner, and your relationship is meant to doom sooner or later.

4. Sabotaging Relationships

People who have a fear of intimacy may sabotage their relationship in many ways. You might get insecure, act suspicious, and accuse your partner of something that hasn't actually occurred. It can also take the form of nitpicking and being very critical of a partner. Your trust in your partner would lack day by day, and you would find yourself drifting apart from them.

5. Difficulties with Physical Contact

Fear of intimacy can lead to extremes when it comes to physical contact. It would swing between having a constant need for physical contact or avoiding it entirely. You might be inattentive to your partner's needs and solely concentrate on your own need for sexual release or gratification. People with a fear of intimacy may also recoil from sex altogether. Both ends of the spectrum lead to an inability to let go or communicate intimately emotionally. Letting yourself be emotionally naked and bringing up your fears and insecurities to your partner may help you overcome this problem.

6. You're Angry - A Lot

One way that the deep, subconscious fear of intimacy can manifest is via anger. Constant explosions of anger might indicate immaturity, and immature people are not able to form intimate relationships. Everyone gets angry sometimes, and it's an emotion that we cannot ignore, even if we want to. But if you find that your feelings of anger bubble up constantly or inappropriately, a fear of intimacy may be lurking underneath. Don't deny these intimacy issues, but instead put them on the table and communicate effectively with the person you are interested in.

Conclusion

Actions that root out in fear of intimacy only perpetuate the concern. With effort, especially a good therapist, many people have overcome this fear and developed the understanding and tools needed to create a long-term intimate relationship.

Chapter 30:

7 Ways To Live Together In Harmony With Your Partner

A harmonious relationship can make a person's life happy and beautiful, but, unfortunately, not all of us are blessed with a harmonious relationship. It is essential to work on your relationship in order to make it work. Creating a harmonious bond between you and your partner can make your relationship more healthy and stable. The dream relationship of everybody is to feel loved, accepted, and respected but to achieve such a relationship, and you need to first work on yourself. You need to make sure that you are doing your best at making your partner feel loved.

Most people nowadays want to find their soulmates, but even when they see their soulmates, they don't have a peaceful relationship; the lack of harmony causes this.

Here are 7 ways to live together in harmony with your partner.

1. Accept Your Partners The Way They Are

The first step to a harmonious relationship is acceptance. It would be best to accept your partners the way they are; distancing them from yourself because of a simple mistake can lead to a toxic relationship. If you choose to love a person and be with them, you need to accept the good and bad in them. As they say that no one is perfect, we all are a work in progress. When you cannot receive your partner the way they are, a harmonious relationship cannot be achieved. It would help if you allowed them to evolve and support them throughout this journey.

2. Be Gentle And Compassionate

When you embody gentleness and compassion, your relationship bond deepens, and there is harmony in the relationship. Instead of jumping to conclusions and reacting dramatically, you need to respond with gentleness and understand your partner's feelings.

Compassion brings grace to a person. To achieve a harmonious relationship, you should give your partner grace to work on themselves, understand, and give them space to evolve and mature. It may take time, but it strengthens a relationship.

3. Expectations Should Be Released

With expectations comes disappointment. Expectations are the unspoken standards you expected your partner to live up to. When your partner does not live up to your expectations, you might feel upset or disappointed, but how can you have such high expectations from your partner about things that are unspoken. Work on letting go of these ideals that the society and your subconscious mind created about how a relationship should be. Release the attachment to situations turning out a specific way. Brace yourself for different outcomes of different situations. Don't expect too much from your partner because your partner, like you, cannot always live up to your expectation.

4. Personal Space In A Relationship

Every human being needs personal space; we often see couples that are always together. It may feel exciting and comforting at first, but everyone needs their personal space to think and function properly. After being with each other with no personal space, one can start feeling suffocated and may behave negatively. It would help if you had time to breathe, to expand, and to look within. To evolve, you need space. Personal space between couples proves that their relationship is healthy and robust.

5. Honesty

Honest communication is not just a factor to achieve a harmonious relationship but also to have any relationship at all. Not being truthful can cause conflicts and problems in a relationship. Moreover, being a liar can be a toxic trait that can cause your partner to end the relationship. But before being honest with your partner, you need to be honest with yourself. Know your true self, explore the good and bad in yourself. Don't hide your mistakes from your partner; instead, be honest and apologize to them before it is too late. Honesty is a crucial factor in achieving a harmonious relationship.

6. Shun Your Ego

Ego and harmony cannot simply go hand in hand; where ego exists, harmony cannot be established. Often by some people, ego is considered a toxic trait. This is the ego that stops a person from apologizing for his mistakes, which can create tension among the couple. The stubbornness to do things your way is caused by ego and can easily result in unwanted scenarios. These are not the components of a healthy relationship. So to establish a harmonious relationship, you should remove ego and learn to compromise a bit. By removing ego, you allow yourself to be more flexible and understanding.

7. Let Go if Unnecessary Emotional Pain

When you keep hurting over old resentments, you convert that pain into toxic feelings that are not good for a relationship. These poisonous feelings can make you make some bad decisions that may result in your partner feeling unsafe around you. This pain can cause you to bury your positives feeling inside. As a result of this, you may feel pessimistic and may exaggerate minor conflicts into something more. A person must let go of this emotional stress and pain. You can let go by going to a therapist or yoga and meditation. Once you have let go of the pain, your heart is now open to a peaceful and harmonious relationship.

To establish a harmonious relationship, you have to accept and understand your partner and work on yourself. Also, work on your radical integrity.

Chapter 31:

10 Signs You're Not Ready For A Relationship

Do you feel the societal pressure to date but can't get yourself into it? Or if you have started dating, ever wondered why your dates go well but you never hear from the person again? Or why despite your best efforts, you can't keep a relationship working? But maybe the problem isn't out there but within yourself.

A relationship can either be the most beautiful thing in your life or the worst. It's not always candlelight dinners and a bed of roses. It requires a strong sense of responsibility and commitment to your significant other. You may feel like you're doing your best, but there are a few factors you should consider that might be keeping your relationships at a distance.

1. **You get overly dependent on people.**

Being emotionally dependent on people sometimes is normal as it is in humans' nature to get reassurance every once in a while. But getting utterly relied on a person to make yourself feel better about yourself can get you nowhere. Your emotions shouldn't be driven by what others might feel or think about you, instead solely by how they will affect you. No one can define your self-worth better than yourself. Try to avoid being too clingy and needy and keep a safe distance from the people you love so you might not annoy them.

2. **Your insecurities reflect on your behavior.**

Whether you have insane trust issues or you feel like you're not good enough, you start showing the signs of your insecurities in your behavior. You start overthinking everything that your partner does; even a slight change in his/her tone is enough to keep yourself wide awake at night. You get incredibly jealous even if your partner does so much as breathe in the direction of someone else. But as they say, that trust is the critical element of a relationship, so why not trust your significant other wholeheartedly and work on yourself to change your pattern of behaviors that may negatively affect your relationship.

3. **You can't stop analyzing your past relationship.**

This is perhaps the most crucial factor as to why relationships usually don't survive. You're still hung up on your ex and compare everything your new partner does to what your old partner used to do. You spend most of your time clinging to your past, daydreaming, or perhaps imagining the situations where you could've right all the wrongs. It's usually not fair to your new partner. Yes, it's not easy to just forget someone and move on, but don't get into a new relationship until and unless you're revived from the old one. Give yourself as much time as you want to murder those old feelings, and when you're done, get yourself out there and enjoy life.

4. You try to change who they are as a person.

Another reason that you can't get yourself into dating is that you're always looking for someone perfect, or if you've already found someone, you're molding them into someone they're not. You're always looking for someone with specific traits that you've written on your bucket list for a long time. You have created an ideal image about your significant other that your start losing your mind if something even minor deviates from it. But isn't love all about accepting someone with all their flaws and weaknesses? Instead, we should try to better ourselves first.

5. You're afraid of a serious commitment.

Maybe the idea of sharing your life and thoughts with someone scares you. You might think, Isn't it too soon to let someone see all of your goods and bad? You haven't fully experienced your life on your own yet. You want to travel the world or do academically better, or maybe you want to spend some alone time. Giving someone your time and energy and being there for them isn't your cup of tea at the moment. The best you can do is be honest and tell them you're not ready for something serious yet.

6. **You don't love yourself enough and have serious self-doubts about yourself.**

We all go through our cynical phases where we feel like we're not worthy of love. But being in that constant phase might affect you terribly. You can't expect someone to love you if you don't even love yourself. Having self-doubts sometimes is normal too, but getting them to a point where your partner might feel irritated and it starts influencing your relationship isn't healthy. We should accept ourselves for who we are, take constructive criticism, and try to be a better person for what it's worth.

7. **You have your walls built up and are emotionally unavailable.**

You don't consider sharing your feelings and thoughts with people. You try to solve every problem independently and isolate yourself from your loved ones now and then. The moment a minor inconvenience happens, or you're upset about anything, you tend to distance yourself from everyone. You don't care enough about other's problems too but rather run from them. No one wants a partner who distances himself; instead, being vulnerable and weak looks attractive. It gives your significant other the confidence that you're true to them with your emotions.

8. **You have poor communication skills.**

Communication is as vital as any other thing when it comes to relationships. If you tend to keep something that bothers you and not express it, you might find yourself in a never-ending pit of overthinking and imagining the worst-case scenarios. Your partner may feel irritated by your constant behavior changes and not knowing the reasons behind them. Talking and sorting out the things concerning you anchors your relationship well and gives you a boost of confidence.

9. **You think that a relationship is your prescription for boredom and loneliness.**

Another primary reason why relationships don't last long these days is that people want to kill their boredom by acquainting with another person. They're bound to put in extra efforts just for the sake of their relationship working out and them not ending up alone. You're willing to make sacrifices just to make the other person happy. This affects your mental state as you're emotionally drained out and always looking for people to cope with your loneliness. But if you aren't happy single, you won't be as comfortable in a relationship too.

10. **You're incredibly inconsistent with people.**

One day you're making them feel like they're on top of the world, and the next day you're crashing them to the ground. You're confused about your feelings for them and are not treating them properly. You might act like the perfect person they can get your hands on, but another moment you might work like you don't even give two cents about them. This might leave your partner in a state of anxiousness and confusion because you're not fully committing to your feelings for them.

In conclusion, it's completely okay not to be in a relationship and not fall victim to societal norms if you're not ready. We should practice self-love before anything else, try to be at peace with ourselves first so that we might be able to bring peace into our partner's life too. I hope these points bring you a new self-awareness and you focus more on the attitude adjustments that will eventually guide you to a path to be ready.

If you found this video helpful, don't forget to like, subscribe, comment, and share this with someone important to you. I hope you learned something valuable today. Take care, have a good rest, and till the next video ☺

CPSIA information can be obtained
at www.ICGtesting.com
Printed in the USA
BVHW040254260122
627128BV00010B/886

9 789814 952583